Happiness Handbook

Being Present Is The Present

By

Phillip Elton Collins

THE ANGEL NEWS NETWORK

HAPPINESS HANDBOOK

ISBN: 0983143366
ISBN: 9780983143369
Contact: info@theangelnewsnetwork.com.

Happiness Handbook
Being Present is the Present:

*Phrases of Presence to Set Us Free
To Be...Happy.*

By Phillip Elton Collins

Dedication

This Happiness Handbook is dedicated to the
I Am Presence innately gifted to us all, a force
from creation that allows us to know who we
are, why we are here, where we are headed,
and how *to be* happy.

"Being present is the most precious part of a person."

—*Saint Germain*

Prologue

One of the most important challenges facing humanity during these times of governmental, religious, corporate, and cultural change is the acknowledgment that support is coming (and has always come) from higher realms outside human experience, awareness, and the mind. We live in a world that thinks that if we cannot see something or prove its existence through our known sciences and senses, it does not exist and cannot be true. New multiverse (as opposed to universe) sciences and the phrases in this book intend to create new truths. Remember that we once thought the world was flat and that the sun revolved around the earth.

While the exact phrases in this book may not exist anywhere else, the teachings and wisdom within these words have existed for eons in this world. I am one of many bringing these forward at this time. All that is here comes from ancient forces (call them what you may) beyond our current reality, which love us deeply and come to us again at present to support our highest good.

Please do not focus on where these phrases come from (unless that brings you further happiness), but focus upon what they are saying, intending, and teaching us. Use your discernment and resonance to apply these phrases in your life if you so desire. If you choose to apply them, you will be able to stand back and watch the happy things that happen! This endeavor is a marriage and mingling of the author's spiritual and energetic training, teaching, and clinical experiences, and the teachings from those ancient, higher realms that remain out of sight.

Preface

No matter where you are at present, I think we would all agree that our personal lives and the world as a whole are going through an extraordinary change. It appears that the old way of doing things just does not work anymore and that we are in the process of creating something new, but we don't quite know what that is going to be or look like yet. We are in process. Maybe the thing that is missing is our "doing" versus our "being." The phrases in this book are pathways to assist you in creating and finding both the new you and the new world and to help you recognize that this process will be one of moving from the "inside out," not the "outside in"—the process of learning how *to be* present.

We often decrease the degree of our happiness as a result of not fully knowing who we are and why we are here. Understanding our purpose in being here and expressing this creates great happiness. The phrases in this book reconnect us with our true being.

There are teachings from higher realms (which have loved and supported us for eons) that say, "the mind that believes is moving back into service of the heart that knows." This means that we are, in fact, we are learning to "think" with our compassionate hearts. This new way of thinking will allow us to transition from our past- and future-oriented way of thinking into the present. Only within the present can we free ourselves from ourselves and assume our destiny to be divine beings of the present, becoming truly happy. By focusing on the present we free ourselves from the lack and limitation, as well as the duality and confrontation, of the past and future. Even the past and the future were once the present. We can only truly evolve as a species and as a planet by mastering the self-empowerment and happiness of the present.

The "pathway phrases" in this handbook are an integration and culmination of higher-realm teachings (call them what you may) and my training and clinical experience as a light ascension therapist/life coach where I assisted others in moving into happiness and a higher frequency of existence. These phrases are an integration of my words with many ancient teachings. These exact words most likely do not exist anywhere else, but their wisdom has existed forever. Repetition is often used since we learn best through it.

While happiness may be stimulated from the outside, happiness is a natural state within us all that can neither be learned nor taught, but it can be awakened. The purpose of this book is to awaken the fulfillment of your happiness from within.

Each phrase in this handbook contains an "energetic" download/upload to assist you in moving into the happiness of the present. Breathe deeply after reading each phrase to allow it to integrate. Each phrase is a separate teaching that joins in community with all the others. You can read them randomly or straight through. Together all the phrases complete a comprehensive blueprint/template for happiness in the present. Open to a page now, and see what the multiverse wishes to teach you and remind you of in the present. There is no right or wrong way to access the presence within each phrase.

I hereby honor and recognize all who have received these similar teachings before me and simultaneously with me. We are all becoming multi-dimensionally connected. Our resonance and discernment will manifest the circumstances of how, when, where, and why we connect with the teaching we need to master. There is nothing either special or unique about anyone bringing these tools into the world.

My previous books *Coming Home to Lemuria, An Ascension Adventure Story; Sacred Poetry and Mystical Messages, To Change your Life and the World;* and *Man Power God Power* all have the same intention as this book: to assist us in waking up and knowing that we are extraordinary beings who deserve to be happy all the time.

Becoming Present is the new and necessary normal.

Phillip Elton Collins

How to Use the Happiness Handbook

(1) With an open heart, recite the following mantra: *I live, move, breath, and have my being within the invincible strength and power of the mighty presence with me.*

(2) Specifically or randomly select a phrase and read it silently or aloud with an open heart.

(3) In order to allow the phrase to integrate into your being, take a deep breath, and on the exhale, drop your jaw, and release the sound AHH. The sound AHH connects us with the same frequency/vibration in which our Presence and happiness lives.

(4) Know within your true sense of self that what you have received in this present moment is exactly what you need in order to be free and happy.

About the Author

My entire life has been one attempt to be happy and to live in the present, but the past and future ruled most of my life until I finally woke up and realized how to better set myself free from the monsters within myself and humanity: the fear, doubt, and ignorance that I experienced through not being Present.

Few of us on this planet maintain and sustain a constant state of Presence, but more and more of us are waking up and releasing ourselves through the innate gift of being Present, which allows happiness.

As a trained light ascension therapist who assists in the balancing of our emotional, mental, and physical bodies, I have reached the point of knowing that being happy in life is about finding, accepting, and connecting solutions to problems in the Present moment. We (humanity and planet) are also, at Present, within what has been called an *ascension process*, breaking down our emotional and mental bodies that have kept us trapped far too long. This breakdown allows a break-through and a connection to this thing called Presence.

Observing our world for almost seven decades, I have seen our belief systems change, knowing that truth is consistent, but truth appears lacking in our world. In fact, much of our world and lives is often based upon untrue beliefs. The innate ability to find Presence within each of us allows us to finally know the truth about ourselves and our world.

The word "Presence" is an attempt to describe an eternal energetic frequency within each of us. We are Presence if we so choose to be. If you don't like the world "Presence," call it something else, but please discover it and be it, and watch what happens to your life as you move into a happier state of being Present.

I believe the purpose of our world is to become Present, and all the words within this endeavor are here to support that truth. My entire personal and professional life is dedicated to us becoming fully Present, allowing us to learn without becoming unhappy.

Time and time again I have seen Presence allow physical beauty to transform into spiritual beauty as we drop our ego-defense masks, heal the "wounded me," and reveal the "healed we" of our cosmic being. Presence allows us to know that happiness and unhappiness are joined together in oneness (made of the same components). It's our connection to time and distance that separate happy from unhappy. The tools (phrases) within this book will allow you to see more deeply into your self-empowerment and into your ability to create a new you and world.

Throughout my professional career I have seen Presence as a heartfelt infinite frequency/wisdom/truth that exposes myself and others to limitless possibilities and probabilities, and creates new lives and communities of equality, harmony, and balance. (Our Presence knows we are not the only ones Present).

Our inner power of Presence reminds us that happiness is a natural state of being which we don't have to earn; we just have to awaken it. Our Presence knows why we have chosen the path of Presence: to give to others and the world what we chose to give ourselves—love.

I bring a diversified background into this endeavor, considering that I am a co-founder of The Angel News Network, a co-founder of The Modern Day Mystery School, a teacher, an author, a poet, a filmmaker and a certified healing arts light ascension therapist who addresses the integration of the emotional, mental, and physical bodies. My professional background also includes extensive management experience at Young & Rubicam Advertising in New York City, international commercial communications skills with innovative filmmaker George Lucas, as well as my role as director of marketing at Industrial Light and Magic, and as a founder of Fairbanks Films with film directors Ridley and Tony Scott.

My previous books are: *Coming Home to Lemuria, An Ascension Adventure Story* (which is currently being adapted into both a stage play and a screenplay), *Sacred Poetry and Mystical Messages, To Change your Life and the World,* containing 116 original poems and higher realm messages, and *Man Power God Power*, an energetic/spiritual reference volume.

Table of Contents

Prologue vii

Preface ix

How to Use the *Happiness Handbook* xiii

About the Author xv

To Awaken Your Presence and Happiness,
See the Following 752 Phrases and Tools
to Support You. xxi

Resources. 377

To Awaken Your Presence and Happiness,
See the Following 752 Phrases and Tools
to Support You

Being Present means joining the **Light Workers** *and the* **Way Showers** *worldwide and walking through our lives in happiness.*

Presence knows exactly how to love self right where you are in each Present moment, allowing us to journey into the unknown without judgment or shame.

Presence, like divine love, is unconditional.

Within true Presence, all pain and suffering is an illusion.

Presence Mantra: I choose no more problems and thus, no more pain for myself or for others because I've had enough of not being Present.

Presence allows us to transmute fear and pain into inner happiness and peace whether or not we are happy.

Our Presence is our ability to move within and to know the happy self is inside to be brought out, not outside to be brought in.

Being Present is knowing that the only way we can receive love from another is by giving it to ourselves first. Are you doing that at Present?

Our Presence knows that our lives may not be becoming exactly what we thought they would. We may be encountering new people and places, just as the old ones are released. Stay open to the possibilities at Present.

Presence is divine responsibility.

All things will eventually return to Presence.
Presence maintains and sustains all.

Our Presence knows our life's purpose is a
process of awakening to our purpose.
Our purpose lives in the Present, waiting to be
discovered just by being who we are. Presence
knows that everything does not happen
instantly; it's a precious, Present process.

Our Presence knows our passion and why we are here. Allow it to tell you and express itself through happiness.

Presence is a formless vibration of freedom and a foundation for all life.

Through Presence we go with the ebb and flow of life, the good and the bad, allowing all things to transform.

Presence means experiencing change as the only possibility by moving into it.

*Our Presence is the key to unlock
our happy future, Presently.*

*Presence teaches compassion for planet Earth
and that all things upon and within Earth's
body are interconnected.*

When we are members of the mind
and not-Present, much of life does not exist;
it remains hidden in the mind.

Presence knows that we are not separate from
ourselves, one another, or the entire world.

Our "comfort zones" are not filled with enough Presence.

Being fully Present is forgiving everything and taking ownership of all that you create in order to learn what you need to learn at Present.

When we can see our thoughts and feel our feelings, we can see the cause and effect in our lives and become Present.

The most magnificent power there is is contained in Presence.

Presence knows we need to give and receive in balance within all Present moments of our lives.

Are some of us still looking into the past and the future and escaping our Presence?

Our Presence allows us to see ourselves in others.

Our Presence knows who we are in each moment of Presence.

Being Present is knowing that we are not our feelings, thoughts, wounds, and defenses.

Once we access our Presence within us, we become self-mastered and can teach the same to others.

Being Present is knowing that the only experience of life is in Presence.

❧

Happiness achieved through Presence is not short-lived like most happiness; it lasts as long as we are Present.

By being Present we can accept pain in life as a learning tool, but not suffering.

Presence reminds us we are moving through a personal process from wounded child to a healed self-mastered adult.

Presence is peeling the onion of the self...deeper and deeper until we hit happiness.

When we are not Present, it is our resistance that creates pain and suffering.

Presence is divinely inspired.

Presence reminds many intelligent and well-educated people that they can often be completely not-Present.

Your life is Present. Be this Presence. Where are you? Be where you are, and allow everything to be you; awaken into the Present.

❦

In Presence, there are no problems and no "dis-ease." Our beliefs hold these in place. Imbalances are instances of Present reality being momentarily out of balance.

Most of the acutely negative events in our lives and world are the results of not being Present.

Being Present is waking up from a long sleep.

Our life, our **beingness,** *exists eternally within the timeless frequency of the Present.*

❦

Presence teaches us that if we love our self-image and reflect it out into the world, we can change the world.

Our Presence wants to know if we can allow Presence onto our life pathway in order to create higher- realms-connected reality.

Presence is not our physical bodies and cannot itself create Presence. Our awareness/ consciousness beyond our physical form is the key. It is challenging for our mental body to know that something unseen beyond the physical body exists, but it surely does. We are now awakening to the unseen worlds becoming Present.

We shall not advance as a species without Presence.

Presence shows us that life can unfold without unhappiness. Look to nature as the example.

Presence teaches us that all other life forms on this planet can show us acceptance and how to surrender to what is.

In order to be president, you need to be Present; this is a new paradigm.

Remember that your physical body houses your Presence; take good care of it.

Our Presence knows that our Presence is enough without having to prove ourselves to anyone in order to be liked or loved.

Presence is not matter, but matter in matter.

⁂

Through Presence we do not need success to have a sense of self.

Our Presence allows our relationship with self to shift into happiness and reflect that within our other relationships.

Presence is a key ingredient within the creation of communities of equality, harmony, and balance through acceptance, compassion, and forgiveness.

Being Present shows us that being unhappy can be the result of our addiction-based comfort zones, which often stimulate our nervous systems.

A new you and a new world are created everyday through Presence.

Being Present is seeing the glass as being completely full in each moment of Presence.

Presence not only allows happiness (things being good), but also an inner peace that can endure no matter whether we are happy or not.

Being Present is knowing that we are here to serve the world through our talents and gifts.

Without Presence all relationships are imbalanced. Remember that the only relationship we are actually having is the one with the self, which is then reflected onto others.

Presence contains self-love and our ability to authentically express who we are.

Presence connects us to our true multi-dimensional nature and to higher realms of energy and truth. We are Presently assisted and are not meant to go it alone.

Presence lets us know that the choices we make require Presence; without Presence there is no choice.

Through Presence the mental and emotional body energies run out.

Our Presence is an infinite frequency from the heart, taking us into infinite dimensions of possibilities and probabilities.

The purpose of this book is for us to become Present.

*Presence knows that separation and duality
live in our mental and emotional bodies.
Acceptance and compassion without judgment
live in our hearts and transform us into oneness
and Presence.*

*The purpose of Presence is to know that
we are the Creator.*

Our Presence asks, "Do I honor and value myself? Who am I? Why am I here? Do I know my life tools at Present?"

❧

Presence knows that I create the new me by just being me, and that going into the unknown allows the next step…and the next and the next, deeper into Presence.

Presence can produce many miracles through the acceptance of the unacceptable.

No one has ever become Present by denying or abusing our visible physical aspects. Presence is a transformative process through the body, not without it.

If you are resonating with a specific teaching, it is because you already have the Presence to recognize Presence in that teaching.

There can be no duality or separation in Presence; you become one with **All There Is.**

Presence is all power, all life, all truth, and all love, and it is ever-Present all the time.

Presence is our divine freedom of choice and of will.

Our Presence activates our passion for being here.

Presence knows that our biological families are filled with separation, isolation, and confrontation. We choose them to learn about what is through *what is not* in the Present.

Being Present is moving from knowing to being you.

Our Presence knows that we are not the only ones Present.

Presence allows us to witness resistance and eventually to know that it has no value.

Lack and limitation need time; they cannot last in the Present—the Present being the true gift of life.

Being Present says, "If you want more time, you'll get it, along with more pain and suffering because the time and pain are inseparable."

Presence asks, "What do I need in the Present moment to be happy?"

Presence teaches that through loving self, we can love another.

If we remove Present pressure from our lives, unhappiness dies.

Death through Presence is the dying of the time-bound self that I think is me.

Presence renders our emotions and thoughts into **energy-less-ness.**

Our Presence is our cosmic transport into our solar system, galaxy, and universe, as well as into the multiverse and beyond...

By using the portals of Presence, we stay linked to All There Is all the time.

Presence is an aspect of the cosmic **divine soul plan.**

Our Presence is all about accepting with compassion, and thus forgiving ourselves for how we are choosing to be happy.

Through our Presence we can accept with compassion and thus forgive what happens within each moment of the Present.

Can we accept with compassion and thus forgive what happens within each moment of the Present? Presence will set us free; are you ready?

Presence is the first step onto the path of not-knowing.

Presence is equality, harmony, and balance.

Be Present.

Resistance through our mental body to becoming conscious produces more unhappiness through not being Present.

Through our Presence, please ask: (1) Who am I being, at Present? (2) Is there a balance of giving and receiving, at Present? (3) What am I feeling, at Present? (4) Where am I, at Present? Answering these questions will put you in your Presence.

Our Presence knows that there are no such things as controlling anyone or anything.

When we apply our freedom of choice and of will from our Presence, we know what is right in that Present moment.

Our Presence knows we are one of two things: either we are happy, or avoiding whatever makes us happy.

Presence supports the fulfillment of our divine soul plan. Did you know you have one?

Being Present is receiving support and guidance from like-minded/like-spirited people and higher realms.

Without Presence we continue our fight for isolation and separation, rather than for oneness.

Presence pauses and asks, "Where are you in this Present moment?" This awareness allows us to make another choice through Presence.

Your individual part of Presence is learning to become Present.

❧

Presence is energy, and energy knows neither distance, nor time. We are all energy.

The more Presence we put into our bodies, the better. Presence reduces or eliminates dis-ease, impedes aging, and creates energy to generate a more evolved self and world.

When we are truly Present, we are our authentic, transparent, and eternal selves, the individuated aspects of Presence.

Presence knows that our purpose in being here is to love and support one another and to be in service to the world.

Presence allows creation to be experienced and expressed through being ourselves.

Our Presence is where we are in this Present moment; when we are aware of it, we are divine.

We are our Presence, or the lack of it, expressing itself Presently.

Presence was born in higher realms,
just like you.

The illusions of time and space are Presence;
these are all one.

Let us value everything, yet let nothing matter because by being Present we have already succeeded.

Presence directs us to like-minded/like-spirited people where our resonance is the same.

Our Presence constantly allows us to review where we are in relation to self and to others, as both change.

Presence shows us that it is not the entire situation that we need to accept; we just need to accept the Present.

Our Presence is constantly asking, "Is being who you are creating happiness?"

Without Presence, what we fear and resist the most is drama and healing.

Our Presence is the space of silence that has always known us.

Presence is the life-force that takes us deeper into the Present.

Our Presence is the aspect of us that allows us to continually know where, who, and why we are. Changing these changes the world.

Presence shows us that all negativity is some form of resistance; what we resist persists.

Our alter ego that lives within our mental body is the monster of humanity who creates fear, doubt, and ignorance. Presence cannot live here, but it can eliminate these aspects.

A good measurement of your level of Presence is how you respond and react to events in your life.

Presence brings all opposites together. It's what makes us one and whole.

At Present, what is the ratio of being to doing in our lives? Presently, how often are we attached to results?

Presence can appear at any moment. Be still and allow it to appear...

Being Present is knowing that we do not need any more suffering in order to wake up.

If we are truly Present, all negativity dissolves. It cannot survive in the Present; it survives in our non-Presence.

Your Presence knows why you have chosen the path of Presence: to give to others and to the world what you chose to give to yourself, love.

Being not-Present rarely offers the most effective solution to anything.

Being Present shows us that being unhappy is insane and unnatural.

The future is Presently connecting with your purpose in being here; this brings happiness.

Our Presence teaches us to let go, to surrender to the unknown, and to accept where we are and that we deserve to be happy.

Consciousness is the user of the power of our Presence.

Presence knows that nothing is what it appears to be.

Our main problem is accepting how truly powerful we are. Let us accept this at Present.

Full Presence means full acceptance.

Our Presence knows that it is essential and that it is our purpose to move onward and upward with all components of our greatness and to bring this out into the world. We are an ever-expanding and growing Present process.

Learn how to feel and think with your Presence (the phrases in this book will allow you to master this).

Resistance to being Present is the reason for most of our personal and global issues. This has created a largely unhappy humanity and world.

Our Presence frees us from our controlling mental body. Presence leaves our unhappy life behind, stopping our search outside the self and showing us we are good enough to be happy at Present.

*Through Presence a great silence awakens
within us, containing limitless peace, love,
and happiness.*

*Being Present supports our intention to change
the self and the world, joining together
like-spirited individuals with a similar purpose.*

People who are truly Present are always Present, using time by being aware, yet free, of it—by honoring the Present.

Our Presence separates the myth of me *from the magnificent* real me.

Our Presence is our deep well of fulfillment through happiness.

Divine power and self-empowerment live within your Presence (sense) of self. Power over another is a lack of Presence masked as force.

As long as our focus is outside of the self, we are not Present. Presence is "inside out," not "outside in."

Perhaps the purpose of the world is to be Present.

*Instantaneous healing occurs through
our Presence.*

*Presence lets us acknowledge that there is
resistance, which is the first step toward
stopping it.*

Enlightenment is being fully Present.

Presence is un-manifested matter; Presence is the energy link to matter.

Pleasure lives outside you, and happiness innately resides within you. Presence and life are processes that are inside out, not outside in.

Our Presence distinguishes between our mental body's conditioning and the truth within our hearts.

Our Presence assists us in making the decision whether to remain within the old way of life or to create a new one.

Becoming-Present is a process every species and planet in the universe/multiverse transitions through...

Positive actions dominate Presence.

Synchronicity often reveals Presence.

Presence is the **god-essence** *in us and in everything.*

Being Present means unrolling the blueprint of our divine soul plan: the reason why we are here.

Presence is our life beginning during every Present moment.

One can find sanity underneath and within insanity through being Present and allowing the healing of self.

Whenever we are watching our mental body, we are being Present; awareness shifts everything.

Our Presence knows that our power and strength do not come from resistance or being right.

Being Present teaches us that unhappiness does not accomplish anything. Unhappiness simply does not work; it attempts to keep things in place.

Presence reveals that true happiness can come through an in-depth examination of self. Presence knows the only relationship we are having is the one with self, which is then reflected onto others.

Being Present means: to release the narcissistic me *and move into the* healed we.

❧

Our Presence asks, "Do you look at the glass as half-empty or half-full?"

In order to shift our consciousness/awareness, we need to be Present.

Our Presence, through its resonance, will manifest our soul family; our lives will be happier with like-minded/like-spirited people around us.

Presence knows that by being vulnerable, we reveal our lack of vulnerability.

∽∾

When we know Presence, it frees us from the illusions of this world; this is truth beyond the seen worlds which we really don't know much about at Present.

Presence allows us to move from
me- *to* we-consciousness.

*When Present we accept what is inside when we
cannot accept what is outside.*

Presence is you becoming **God-as-you.**

*There is never a Present in your life
that is not Present.*

Presence is an essential and powerful tool being used within our ascension process into higher realms at Present.

Presence teaches us to break down (in order to break through) the energy of old conditioning in our mental body and to clear and to cleanse all our energy through our hearts.

Our Presence knows that we must first judge and shame ourselves before we can do this to anyone else; being Present prevents this.

The only way to change what is outside us is to commit through being Present to change ourselves inside.

Presence is the hand of creation creating you, the most amazing miracle of all.

Our Presence fills our emptiness and dissolves our fear of being alone. Through our Presence we learn to love self enough to be alone without being lonely.

Our Presence is the vehicle for leaving our unending drama behind, dropping the mask of unhappiness, and allowing ourselves and others to know that we are happy individuals.

Try contacting and connecting with your Presence each night before you go to sleep; during your sleep you'll put your Presence to good use for tomorrow...

Being Present is knowing that you can never go back to the old comfort-zone behaviors.

As long as we stay connected to our emotional and mental bodies, we can never know a complete sense of Presence.

Silence is a key ingredient in Presence. Hear the wisdom in the void that contains all probabilities and possibilities, free of emotions and thoughts.

Many people die never feeling that they lived. Don't wait; start at Present to live life fully. Be Present and enjoy being.

Being Present is discovering what you have been hiding and are Presently ready to bring out into the world.

Within Presence we are moving from a Present of possibility to a Present of probability, and from a Present of wondering to a Present of fulfillment where our life becomes happy.

Without Presence, our life and world can be seen as a fearful, hostile, and fragmented place.

Presence heals all past and present life wounds and the defenses created around those wounds.

Presence knows that without a change in self, little in life will change; life is an inside-out, personal process.

Presence will prevent us from fighting for power to be right. It will allow us to move from our mental body to our heart space.

To be Present is to "just be."

Our Presence does not have to look outside the self for gratification or validation.

Presence is here to facilitate a new golden age.

*Focusing on the past and future increases
the physical body's aging. Be Present,
and stay more youthful.*

Presence is activated through breath, sound, motion, and feeling our emotions.

Presence allows us to stop seeking outside the self; all we need is within us. Stop looking!

In non-Presence, life exists in the past and the future, never the Present.

Through Presence, when action is required, you will respond rather than react.

Forgiveness is a great gift of Presence. Only Presence can forgive, not our emotional or mental bodies.

Divine love surrounded by Presence moves us beyond our emotional and mental bodies at warp speed.

Be it and do it within Presence or not at all; for without Presence, there can be no authentic being and doing.

Our Presence knows that life is not an arbitrary act on our part, but a lifelong Present experience intended to bring happiness.

Our Presence teaches our minds and emotions that it's all about what is rather than what is not.

Our power-of-Presence is creation holding our hand, a divine connection indeed!

All that you physically, mentally, and emotionally think you are is a misperception of your Presence, which is eternal.

All that is Presently being said in this book is you listening to you.

*Presence includes living the life that
you say you want.*

*Presence is undifferentiated until it connects
with our soul.*

The Present is all that really exists.

Try reviewing each day, at the end of that day, through our Presence, releasing any and all shame or judgment. How would that feel?

As long as we think the mind is in control, it will rule our lives. Our Presence is our freedom from our mind, for it lives outside the mind.

Presence teaches us that we are much more than our physical bodies, emotions, or thoughts.

Being Present teaches us that we can always become more Present.

Without Presence we are often attempting to arrive somewhere that we are not. We can never be happy with this way of being.

Presence defies the herd mentality and allows you to be uniquely you; the multiverse would be incomplete without you.

Our Presence reminds us that our life is one of constant shifts and changes all taking place within us during the Present.

Our Presence knows that resisting lack and limitation (what we resist persists) will keep us in the illusion and delusion of life and in a state of unhappiness. Only what is Present is real.

Our Presence allows us to accept with compassion where we are in each Present moment without shame, blame, or judgment; without Presence, we first judge ourselves before judging others.

Presence allows self-mastery, self-knowledge, and becomes a way of showing for others who need us.

❦

Our Presence knows that we shall shift back and forth between the believing-mind and the knowing-heart until we remain in our heart.

Through Presence we can achieve ownership of our life and eliminate victimhood.

Becoming Present is knowing that there are other ways to enlightenment rather than suffering.

Our Presence is our deep place within us that can never be reached by external events.

Our Presence is the clear and concise picture we intend to manifest.

*Being Present allows us to know that
attachments and addictions are refusals to
acknowledge and shift through our pain.
Presence sets us free from pain and prevents
suffering (long term pain).*

*Our Presence constantly raises our resonance
and vibration into happiness; it knows nowhere
else to be or to go.*

Presence knows that you always get a second chance.

❧

When Present, an intelligence much greater than our mental body comes into play.

Love turns to its opposite (hate) without Presence.

Presence is your ticket from a universe to a multiverse, in order to discover that you are a multi-dimensional being.

With Presence we live in the "what is" rather than the "what is not." This ends all resistance and addiction dreams.

At Present, our emotions and thoughts create our reality all the time. Shall we Presently make another choice?

Our Presence knows that we are here to put ourselves into action by knowing who we are in the Present through commitment.

Being fully Present can allow a deep inner peace which moves beyond sadness into sacred serenity and happiness.

Only the Present can free us from the past and the future; more past and future cannot free us. What is essential is to connect with the power of Presence right now.

Presence allows us to trust ourselves and thus others; this reduces separation and isolation.

Presence knows we do not need to validate or gratify ourselves, but just to simply be who we are.

Within being Present, we move from the insanity of the "wounded me" into the healed, sane consciousness of the "we."

Our Presence allows us to integrate our feelings into the Present, allowing us to be who we are and happy.

Presence says, "Why not decide to be happy now, no matter what?"

*Let us have compassion for all who lack
Presence. This includes ourselves.*

*Our Presence knows that it is about our being,
not our doing. Am I Present at Present?*

Acceptance of what is is fully being Present.

Presence is an upload from our Creator.

When we are Present in our mental body, it becomes more conscious, letting us use it, rather than it using us.

Through Presence we know it is essential to know what we are feeling, to know our needs, and to know where we are in the Present.

Our Presence knows that when we stop looking outside ourselves for solutions and focus within, we can embrace our talents and gifts, bring them out into the world, and be happy.

If our mental bodies are not supported by Presence, the likelihood of unhappiness is high.

Presence allows us to fully experience the unknown.

Why do we demand that life should make us happy and become sad when our expectations aren't met? Suppose that we could be happy no matter what, just by Presently being happy.

Presence frees us from the prison of our thoughts and emotions.

We can never feel lonely by being alone with our Presence.

When we enter the Present, change can come about without much doing, just with being.

Our Presence wishes for us to know that our life is a constant clearing and cleansing process, lead by our resonance and discernment. Out with the old, in with the new...

Our Presence knows what brings us the greatest happiness and how to share it with others.

Our Presence allows us to know our truth, speak our needs, and set our boundaries within each moment of the Present in order to be and remain happy.

In life, focus on the Present; the solutions will come when the future becomes Present.

Once you are Present with Presence, you are Present.

Our Presence is an energy radiating from within our heart, showing us who we really are.

Presence is a personal process of accepting the divine you.

Within Presence there is a deep- seated happiness that moves beyond anything good or bad.

Our Presence has always asked us to check back within ourself through our heart-space as things change; then Presence can re-connect us with our true self. Be patient; you are building a new you at Present.

Presence emanates and resides within our hearts.

Our Presence is a process of knowing we are here to serve one another and our world.

You cannot have an argument with a fully Present person. To argue is to be in our mental body; a Present person works from within his or her heart.

By becoming the quiet observer of our Present lives, we master self and life.

The activation of our soul plan occurs through Presence.

❧

Without Presence, the mental body housing the alter ego becomes a major problem.

Within our final destination, Presence will become everlasting.

When there is no Presence in the masses, there is mass unconsciousness, mass resistance, and drama—this sounds like our world today.

There is only one point in actually accessing life: the Present.

In Presence there is no judgment of the Present.

Presence teaches us that dis-ease is not the issue; we are the issue, as long as the mental body is in control.

We find Presence the moment we know that we don't need to look for it.

In the being of our Presence, we know we are a formless, timeless being that is currently maintaining and sustaining our physical bodies.

Our Presence wants to know: (1) Is being unhappy your "comfort zone"? (2) Do you fear the unknown? (3) Do you see yourself as good or worthy enough to have something else?

Presence allows new choices.

❦

The unseen and seen of Presence are one;
the energetic essence of everything and
everyone is one.

Without Presence the unhealed alter ego within our mental body runs and often sabotages our life by creating duality and separation.

When we stay Present with our entire being, we bring light into every aspect of our being.

Presence releases us from trying to figure things out, and allows us to see life as an organic "grace and ease" process.

When we move into the Present, we can feel the interconnectivity of everything. Let us attempt to remove ourselves from the concept of time as often as possible; live in the Present and see how different our lives can be!

Happiness is a Present-process from inside out, not outside in.

❧

Presence knows that our new soul families are created from the healed me through focusing outward—first me, then the group, and then the world...

Our Presence knows what brings us the greatest happiness, raises our frequency, and brightens the world; our Presence is constantly showing us our way to happiness.

When we set ourselves free from the emotional, mental, and physical, we are divinely Present. This is rare, but possible.

Presence reveals that intellectual agreement from our mental body is often a belief that can change.

Our Presence is Presently asking us to embody (to be) our essence (talents and gifts), revealing to us the meaning, value, and purpose of our being here.

*All the wisdom through Presence in this book
is from higher-frequency realms to assist us in
freeing ourselves from ourselves by being happy.*

*Presence supports us in truly valuing ourselves
and others.*

Through your Presence, you are moving deeper and deeper within, to the core of your heart, and feeling your feelings as you ascend into happiness.

∾

Being Present is knowing that we are here to shift the energies within ourselves in order to evolve individually, thus helping the world evolve.

Presence allows for the discovery of who you are and why you are here through an organic personal process that can come about through grace and ease.

There is Presence in everything; it is the glue of creation.

*In the state of Presence through nonresistance
and unconditional love, we no longer accept
unhappiness.*

*Presence knows that happiness comes from that
which resonates in our life. This will raise our
vibrations and create more happiness.*

Being Present is responding, rather than reacting, to life, which allows a loving Presence and a space for you and others to be who you are.

When we are not connecting and knowing Presence, we are often creating drama, which can become an addiction and overtake our total identity.

Through Presence we shall connect with our truth, needs, and boundaries.

Presence is filled with the "space substance" of life.

The truth of our being will come when we eliminate the mental body's attachment to the past and the future. Then, we shall set ourselves free in the present.

The power-of-Presence dissolves the past and the future's pain.

Being Present is consistently living in each Present-to-Present Presence.

Presence allows us to know that happiness and unhappiness are joined together in oneness. It's our dimensions of time and distance that separate them.

Being Present is knowing and defending your divinity in all ways. We are all aspects of the sacredness of life.

Presence teaches us that when we can accept what is in every Present moment, then we will be fully conscious and awake, and thus, Present.

When Present, we cease having separation from or conflict with self and others.

Presence stops resistance; what we resist persists.

Every Presence creates its Presence.

Presence cannot harm you, others, or the planet.

*Presence is part of feeling out of control
and within the chaos of the creative process.
Presence knows that we really do not
control anything.*

*Through being Present, we can see the
interconnectivity of all things, not just by seeing
the other, but by **being** the other.*

*Energy from our mental body can become
Present when we use our mental body rather
than letting it use us.*

❧

*When your sense of self and of being human
becomes conscious, then you are Present;
you are alive.*

When we are Present, we are in the only moment there is, then, in the next moment, and the next and the next...

Divine Presence is our true nature. The **I Am Presence** *is the* **merkaba** *that manifests our true being.*

Presence shows us that the Present is more valuable than the past.

Your higher-self-being is always whole and complete in the Present.

Imagine, if all our governmental, religious/
spiritual, and corporate leaders were Present,
what a different world we would have.

You can only fully love yourself, and thus others,
through being Present.

Our Presence knows that we are all teaching what we need to learn, the teacher being the student and the student being the teacher. Combining these we learn what we came here to learn.

"No-thing" can exist without Presence; everything comes from Presence.

Presence is the fuel of transition and transformation.

❧

Fear, doubt, and ignorance (the mobsters of humanity) dissolve in the Presence of Presence.

Being Present is connecting with like-minded/ like-spirited people.

Within Presence we are faced with choices: Do I stay where I am in the old, repeating the old, or do I move into the new, always in the Present?

There is nothing we can ever do or achieve that will get us closer to Presence than at Present.

Our Presence knows that the most empowering way to shift from our mind to our heart is to simply ask, "What do I love? Where is my gratitude?"

Being Present allows us to heal wounds and to no longer need ego defenses which prevent us from being Present.

Presence is always having us change how we relate to self, others, and our endeavors, for we are never the same in each Present moment.

*Our Presence knows we are Presently within
an ascension process that is creating a higher
frequency of existence; this is why we are here
at Present.*

*Presence knows that anything that is not true
happiness disappears like it never existed.*

Our Presence knows we can live our truth; this is available to us always at Present.

Our Presence allows us to feel our feelings through breathing deeply with sound and motion. This allows the energy to move through us rather than staying within. Life is breath, sound, and motion.

*Our Presence is our gift to ourselves. How are
you using it at Present?*

Presence is the **manifestor** *in our lives.*

Our Presence (within all advanced civilizations) knows that there is no time other than the Present.

Your Presence knows that we are here to create unity and that balance, equality, and Presence are the same thing.

Presence is the tool to release the old habits, patterns, rituals, and attachments that keep you unhappy.

❦

Being Present is being aware that I can't— and I don't have to—do it alone. I can create community.

We can only truly forgive by being Present. We cannot forgive what is in the past. Forgiveness takes place in the Present.

❦

Being Present allows us to be more compassionate, forgiving, accepting, humble, true, and free.

Bringing breath into our body activates Presence.
Breath, sound, and motion=Presence.

In each moment of the Present, it is our divine
right to receive all the universe/multiverse has
to give; only the un-Present self can prevent this.

To fully experience love is to increase the awareness/frequency of our Presence. This allows the vibration of our Presence to transcend the painful, selfish self and to reveal our unconditionally loving soul just being itself.

Presence allows us to know the highest good in what we think is bad.

Our Presence empowers us and releases all that does not serve our highest good or that is not a good use of our energy.

Presence teaches us that what's left after our so-called death is our Presence.

*Surrendering to the unknown is scary
without Presence.*

*Divine love is as rare as fully Present
individuals.*

*Presence allows physical beauty to transform
into spiritual beauty.*

*Being Present is not about separation nor
confrontation; it is about shifting your vibration
to a higher resonance that allows more Presence.
Then, this new Presence becomes your Present
truth and loves you and others exactly
where you are*

Presence teaches us that our perception of the world is a reflection of our Presence.

Our Presence knows that others wish to be spoken to the same way that we speak to ourselves, Presently.

*Everything will eventually return to Presence
from whence it came.*

*Without access to the power-of-Presence, we lose
our freedom of choice.*

Our Presence often asks, "What resonates for me? What does not?" We can now use our discernment and move deeper into Presence.

❧

Presence was never created. It just is.

Presence allows energy to emit from our heart, raising the essence and vibration that is us.

Presence teaches us that there can be no lasting happiness in what we do, possess, or achieve; all that exists always passes through change. Happiness can be eternally achieved through Presence.

Being Present allows us to learn without being unhappy.

Our Presence knows that each one of us has a unique path to follow...

Our Presence knows that the old must be released to make way and move forward into the new.

Being Present is being in We-Consciousness leaving the nasty me behind.

Through Presence we can connect to the higher realms of our creation.

Presence allows us to become alchemists, transforming fear into love, darkness into light, pain into awareness.

The essence that burns deep within us is our Presence. It moves out from our hearts with an energy to express the **divine you.**

Presence allows us to forgive every moment, especially the Present; then, we no longer have to forgive anything later on.

When there is dis-ease, attempt not to give it any past or future; allow it to transport you in the Present, and then, see what appears...

Being Present is moving from Me- to We-Consciousness. Am I ready to serve my world through all that is being said in this handbook of tools?

The awakening of our Presence can be gradual or sudden. What do you choose?

When we know we are not Present, we become Present/aware/conscious.

Our sense of Presence is our true sense of self.

Presence teaches us that resistance to change is a sure way to suffering; nothing is forever, except for our eternal, Present spirit.

Presence is Oneness Consciousness, knowing that we are one with love.

Within each moment of Presence, let us not forget to ask: "What do I need? Am I able to give myself what I need in the Present?"

Presence is constantly asking us to move forward in living the life we say we want and in manifesting our purpose in being here.

Is your nervous system addicted to the drama of not enough Presence?

Being Present is knowing why you are here.

Presence allows us to see that all that we create in life (illness, accidents, etc.) are teaching tools that we own.

Presence teaches us to give to ourselves what we need (not want) in each Present moment. What do you need at Present?

When all your Presence is Present, you are Present; you are then in your sense of self, being Present.

Presence is resonant causation; what we resonate with, we create.

Presence is man-power becoming god-power; there are Presently energies and forces in place like never before, insuring and assisting our Presence.

Our Presence is the truth of us at Present.

When truly Present, we experience the miracle of surrender, transforming acute suffering into divine happiness.

Our Presence is filled with resonance and discernment.

We have been frozen in a state of not being Present far too long. Many of us are becoming Present in order to create a new self and a new world.

Being Present is being your best, even though that changes from Present to Present.

Presence is made up of all that is, all that is not, and all that ever will be.

Presence is the soul awakened in us.

Our Presence is forever moving us from our believing minds to our knowing hearts.

Being Present involves celebrating you and being happy all the time by knowing who you are and why you are here.

Our Presence will question why we may continue relationships that do not serve our highest good while asking us to consider moving away from them, at Present.

Our Presence asks, "__Am__ I using my talents and gifts to be happy? Or am I giving to get? Or a little of both?"

Presence is us moving ourselves from childhood into adulthood.

Our Presence knows why we are here. Are you ready to access it?

Presence is the common sense to move into something or someone else when necessary.

There is "no-thing" you need to know to be present. You are Presence.

❦

Our Presence is always integrating us into higher frequencies of energy that are reflecting the planet's process of creating a new paradigm of happiness.

Being Present is knowing that problems and solutions are aspects of Presence to be accepted and connected at Present. Problems are products of our mental body and need past and future to flourish. Problems cannot sustain themselves in the Present. Our mental body needs past and future to flourish. Problems cannot sustain themselves in the Present. Think about it; its true!

Presence allows us to accept that whatever we create comes into our lives a learning tool.

Being Present is breaking all illusions in our lives that are no longer the best use of our energy or that serve our highest good in the Present.

❧

When we are Present, we can be aware of our mental body, see it, become free of its control, and begin to know that we are not it.

In Presence, I surrender without resistance. One iota of resistance will prevent Presence.

Breathe with sound and motion; this will assist in maintaining Presence. Be Present with your breath.

Our Presence knows that our unseen aspects of self are our most important aspects; we are moving from believing that the seen is all there is, to knowing the unseen.

Our Presence knows whether we are committed to being Present or not.

We cannot be in or out of our physical body without being Present; we cannot exist without being Present...we just have to become aware of it.

~

We're all going to end up at the same glorious, Present destination; it's just a matter of how and when.

The opposites of Presence are lack, limitation, duality, confrontation, pain, dis-ease and death.

Our Presence allows us to tell ourselves and others who we are and why we are here, through valuing and honoring our happy selves.

Our Presence allows us to know that the truth of our life lies within our knowing heart and through feeling and releasing our emotions.

Through Presence we move from childhood into adulthood. Being Present is a process of moving inside out, not outside in.

Most of our negative emotions, including fear, doubt, anger, and nonforgiveness, are products of the past and of not enough Presence.

Presence knows you've always been ready to join your happiness-energy with others as a true sense of self based upon love.

Through Presence we realize that the old no longer works. We need newness even if we don't exactly know what that is at Present.

Presence is your true frequency and vibration being you.

Presence is the vehicle to communities of equality, harmony, and balance.

Presence supports our moving into the intersection of the new and the unknown.

At Present, is there a balance of giving and receiving in your life, creating happiness?

❦

To know Presence is to know that it exists in every other person.

Many people arrive at a sense of self through everything but Presence: a false Presence is filled with ego, belief systems, duality, and relationships that have nothing to do with true Presence.

❧

Your options at Present are to: (1) distance yourself, (2) make another choice, or (3) accept what is. All these will create happiness.

*Becoming Present and happy is a process
that begins with releasing layers of wounds
and defenses from our minds and emotions,
transitioning into the purity and truth
of our selves.*

*Being Present is a balance of giving and
receiving (love).*

Presence is a doorway that love can enter.

Is there joy and ease in your life, Presently?
Honor the Present moment and see
what happens!

Presence transmutes a lack of peace into peace.

*Our Presence wishes us to be grateful for being
Present and for knowing why we are here.*

*Bad things happen due to a lack of Presence;
no one chooses them.*

❧

*Our Presence is our life to live, to give, to
receive, to be and to accept the process
of that life.*

Presence teaches us not to become attached or addicted to anything outside the inner self.

Presence, like martial arts, knows not to resist the opponent's force. Surrender to overcome. Doing nothing within inner Presence is a mighty healer and transformer of people and events.

Presence is our direct connection to spiritual dimensions.

To surrender to not-knowing is to accept Presence unconditionally; in the void of not-knowing lies everything.

It is the quality of our Presence that will determine our Present and future.

Before we are fully Present, we often rock back-and-forth between being Present and not.

Our Presence is an essential part of the "we" of the world, not the "me."

⁂

The human mind is ruling humanity at Present, but Presence rules the planet, solar system, universe, and multiverse.

Presence is not elsewhere; it has always been here and in the Present.

Presence is an inseparable aspect of timelessness and formlessness, one unified field from which all that exists derives its being.

*We cannot be unhappy and fully Present at the
same time; resisting what is Present creates
unhappiness.*

*Our Presence is the light inside us that sees us
through the darkness, the unknown journey.*

Presence is a force of creation and a force of being, which teaches us to wake up and love.

❦

Presence does not allow unhappiness in any portion of our inner being.

Our Presence knows that it is essential for us to be impeccably accountable to our word, in order to move from deceit into truth and happiness.

Presence is the most God-like thing happening!

Presence knows we are enough when we love ourselves Presently.

To be Present is to not involve the mental and emotional bodies in their acts of shaming, blaming, and judging.

We can always be in contact with Presence because we are it.

✎

If we are at Present being Present, we are waking up and are ready to really remember why we are here.

Presence is Oneness.

*Presence is born in nothing and returns to nothing; it is really not in, but **of**, the world.*

True Presence is a state of freedom from self and others, as well as from lack, limitation, fear, duality, need, our mental and emotional bodies, time and distance.

Presence allows us to move into the transition from old to new through an integration period... we are in process...

*Surrendering, or doing nothing within Presence,
entails acute alertness and inner nonresistance.*

⤙

*The change in consciousness can come through a
complete surrender to not-knowing in
the Present.*

We change almost every aspect of ourselves by becoming fully Present; through magnifying our Presence and taking it deeper into our being, we may connect with the divine in each of us.

Our Presence knows that situations are not the cause of unhappiness; our lack of ownership of what we create (in order to learn) is the cause of unhappiness.

When everything else is removed or is gone, your Presence eternally remains.

Presence knows that when there appears to be no way out, there is always a way **through** *by focusing on our feeling and releasing it.*

*Presence teaches us that emotion is the
expression of feeling.*

*True Presence goes beyond empathy and
sympathy into knowing we are one.*

The heart is the organ of Presence.

Presence is the key to transformation; complete Presence requires acceptance and compassion and thus, forgiveness. Presence is our inner light transforming everything into itself.

To become Present, we need to reclaim the true unseen aspects of self. A simple way to do this is to stop thinking that we know it all.

❧

Presence is a frequency from which you receive love by releasing whatever it is you still need, in order to achieve happiness.

Presence allows humanity to know we are here;
many creatures on this planet do not have
Present awareness of this.

Presence is our internal "gyro system," guiding
us toward our true being.

Our Presence knows that change is all there is. Happiness comes from the acceptance of change without control.

❧

The mental body, Presently left to its own devices, cannot express the divine.

Our Presence knows that when we accept what is within ourselves, this will bring light into the darkness.

Being Present is you experiencing yourself being god, being itself.

Presence is the source and energy of all life.

❦

Presence is a unified whole; nothing is separate in Presence.

The word "Presence" is not Presence. You are if you so choose to be. If you don't like the word Presence, call it something else. But please be it.

❦

Presence knows that all we ever wanted or avoided is ever-Present to bring us happiness. Are we ready to embrace our Present happiness?

Presence is knowing when we are walking our soul path into not-knowing; when creating the new me and the new world and realizing that being in control is not part of the process, we become happy.

When we are Present, we are neutral to where we are at Present, knowing there is no right or wrong, just choices from which to learn.

Our Presence knows our passion, purpose, and reason to be here.

Our Presence knows the innate power that lies within us. We are creators of our lives and our world through Presence.

Loss of being Present is the loss of our very being.

Being Present means: ending the struggle to endure life.

Our Presence reminds us that our happiness is contained in knowing who we are and why we are here: our Present purpose!

Most people are unaware of their Presence. They think they exist, but without Presence there is nothing.

Through our Presence, our nonphysical body is the pathway to our true eternal being of light and love.

Presence is the key essence in creating a new world paradigm completely different from the old one.

Our Presence knows we hold the key to open the door to bring Presence out into the world.

Presence is forever. Our emotions, thoughts, and even physical bodies have short life spans.

Presence is a mighty transformer of people and circumstances. When circumstances don't change, your Presence allows acceptance and happiness in the Present.

Presence reveals that beliefs can change and that truth is consistent; our world and lives are Presently based upon many untrue beliefs.

*In what ways are we in denial of the Present?
What am I feeling at Present? Am I happy being
who I am at Present?*

All things are held in place by Presence.

All Presence originates from the same source, your connection to Source/All There Is/Creator/ God.

Presence knows that we are here to be in service to the world.

To be Present, conscious, and awake is to observe what is happening inside of you, not outside of you.

When we become Present, we are ready to transmute and transform our lives; old habits and patterns die, and we create new paradigms for ourselves and the world.

Presence allows us to express our talents and gifts in service to all, which is the reason we are here.

Our Presence recognizes that we have always been good and worthy enough to have the happy life we say we want.

Our Presence knows that all aspects of our selves are interrelated; nothing is separate. Our being, our doing, our talents and gifts, our who, our why…are all part of being Present.

Presence asks the question, "Is there any happiness in the attachment to drama and glamour we create?"

Our Presence has always existed and yet is more accessible at Present.

❦

Being Present reveals that we humans are the only beings on this planet that experience unhappiness, and through this, we destroy self, others, and our planet.

At the moment of death, we become completely Present, if at no other time in our life.

Presence knows that there is no death and that there is nothing to fear.

Through Presence there is nothing to do,
just to be.

Being Present with our emotional, mental, and
physical bodies keeps us Present. What are
you feeling at Present? What are you thinking
at Present? What is your physical body
experiencing at Present?

Presence opens a door to a personal process to know who you are and why you are here. Did any of your past teachers ask you who you are?

The past and future were once the Present. So the eternal Present is actually where we live our lives. When we think of the past and future, we are doing it in the Present.

Presence constantly releases our attachments, addictions, and expectations of the past and the future, and allows the Present to be the focus of our life.

Our Presence knows that that with which we resonate manifests and is called resonant causation.

Being Present is essential to self-mastery. Mastery and Presence live in our hearts, not in our minds.

Our Presence allows the full use of our discernment and resonance in the choices we make through our freedom of will, which is always Present within Presence.

*Presence is access to a formless higher realm
that knows neither time, nor distance.*

*Presence shows us that any imbalance in our life
can reveal happiness/enlightenment when we
eliminate resistance.*

Presence assists in gathering together like-spirited individuals in communities of equality, harmony, and balance that create more Presence; being Present helps keep our wounds and defenses out of the group.

Presence is nonresistance to life by allowing life to live within, and outside of, you.

*Our Presence wants to know all the things
we have gratitude for within our Present life.
Gratitude=abundance=happiness.*

*Being Present is knowing that we are living at a
most important time for ourselves and the world.*

Pain/suffering fuels itself and can become an addiction; Presence is the antidote.

Being Present is knowing that it is time for us to receive love…and knowing in the Present that this comes from ourselves, first and foremost.

This book is a tool-box filled with tools to teach us how to be Present.

Presence reveals our feelings and our truth in each Present moment.

Our Presence identifies the new soul families we create through resonance and discernment.

❧

Presence is saying, "It is time to love you and to be happy." Can you hear it?

Presence shows us the best use of our energy and what serves our highest good. Presence shows us where the old no longer works.

It is always up to us how we choose to use our Presence through our freedom of choice and of will.

When we are Present our wounds, ego defenses, and false masks no longer apply.

Presence, the unseen, can bring the seen into your life.

Pure Presence is complete awareness that sets us free from the wounded physical world and allows us to create a new healed self and world.

Do you know who you are, at Present? Do you know why you are here, at Present?

Have you noticed how much our sense of self is related to the past and the future and not to the Present?

Our Presence is evolving along with the multiverse. It's all interconnected. Everything, including you, is growing and expanding throughout eternal Presence.

Our Presence knows who we are and why we are here; listen in the silence, and it will tell us (again).

Our Presence allows us to connect to the conviction and commitment necessary to create happiness.

We cannot find ourselves in the past or future. We really only exist in the Present. All else is illusion and delusion.

Our Presence knows what we love, and do not love, about our self; knowing and loving self is the key to happiness.

Being Present is employing unconditional love filled with acceptance and compassion, composed of our truth, needs, and boundaries.

Our Presence allows us to differentiate between knowing who we are through our mental body and our self-love and heart-space; one can create duality, the other oneness.

Presence knows that imbalances have nothing to do with who we truly are or why we are here.

Being Present is choosing to live in a state of Presence, rather than in time.

Our inner Present body can and does affect our outer physical body in balancing and healing imbalances.

❦

Our Presence supports everything with which we strongly resonate—people, places, and things—and teaches us to be Present with them.

By being Present, we are being God's messenger as Presence.

❧

To know you are not Present is a great gift.

Our Presence knows that before we can balance giving and receiving, we need to know what we have to give and need to receive.

When our world ends, Presence will still exist to create other worlds.

When there is not Presence in our lives, we can create drama by feeling alone, sorry for ourselves, and resentful. We allow the past or the future to rule our lives and prevent Presence.

Presence manifests in others like you. We entrain to the highest frequency within our Presence.

Being Present is healing all that we need to heal.

Presence is the nourishment of love.

Presence is beyond the human mind,
but not the heart.

Presence eliminates victimhood and replaces
it with ownership; taking ownership of all we
create sets us free to be Present.

Non-Presence is the livelihood of unhappiness.

Without Presence, when two unhealed mental bodies collide, there is war.

Our Presence wishes us to be happy and grateful for being ourselves.

Presence teaches us that everyone's path of receiving and giving love is the same.

"To thine own self be true, and know thyself,"
speaks our Presence.

❧

Your Presence knows: you are not your job,
your stuff, your belief systems, your knowledge/
education, your body, your gender, your religion
or anything else you think you are. The secret of
life is dissolving all that you are not, allowing it
to die. Then, you can know that you can never
die, for you are a Present, eternal being!

Through Presence we see the universal, interconnected life- and death-cycles of all things; one cannot exist without the other.

Presence is death's transition and ticket into immortality. Through Presence we know that we never die.

*When we become Present, we can become aware
of our mental body; then we can see it, be free of
its control, and begin to know that we are not it.*

❧

*Our Presence knows exactly what we have to be
and to do in order to create a new us
and a new world.*

You can never lose Presence once you become aware of it. It is not dependent on anyone else other than you.

❧

If your life is unhappy, separate out the Present, and surrender to it; then you can no longer resist or react.

Presence is All There Is.

Presence is the divine aspect within us.

*By holding the vibration/frequency of Presence,
we wake up and become conscious, eliminating
negativity.*

*We do not have to wait for someone else to
become Present before we do.*

In Presence there can be no duality, separation, or confrontation…there is only All There Is.

Creation is Presence.

Presence joins the physical with the spiritual.

❧

Presence is love, loving you.

Being Present is a balance of giving and receiving.

Presence knows that we are bound to this world, yet are preparing to break free...

Presence knows that reality is not based upon doing, but rather upon being. What is your ratio of being to doing?

The fastest way to wake up is to be Present.

Our Presence lets us know when we are Present and ready to know why we are here.

❧

Being Present is knowing that surrender is not defeat; it is wise to yield to opposition. What we resist persists.

Presence knows that the illusions of our physical body and of death are the same illusion.

❧

Presence + Acceptance= transmutation.

Our Presence teaches us how to trust ourselves. Through acceptance of and compassion for this trust, we gain further happiness.

Knowing who you are means that you can just be you in the Present all the time.

Our Presence knows that we are unique, individuated aspects of the universe and the multiverse, and that they would be incomplete without each of us.

Presence always accepts the Present.

*Happiness through both resonance and Presence
can spread like a virus.*

*Without Presence we are filled with the illusion
of separation.*

Our Presence is constantly showing us why there are things in our life that create unhappiness and how to release them...

When we feel or really see something, we are Present.

Our Presence is the tool-box that contains all the tools we need to receive life.

Our Presence allows us to know and value ourselves within each moment of Presence, knowing that change can come within each Present moment.

*Presence frees us from the dichotomies of good/
bad, like/dislike, love/hate and right/wrong.*

*Are you ready to be Present and to release the
illusions of the past and the future that have
kept us trapped in lack and limitation
far too long?*

Presence can balance the masculine and feminine energies. The imbalance of these is the cause of all duality, separation, and confrontation.

Presence is giving up the separated self.

Presence teaches us that the more we seek happiness through things, the more it will elude us. Things can give us pleasure for a time. Nothing can give us sustained happiness. Happiness comes from the inside out, not from the outside in.

Being Present means: loving myself right where I am at Present.

Presence is a manifestation of knowing on a **soul level.**

❧

Presence knows that your new, happier life is filled with the impeccable integrity of your word and with your love of self, which is reflected in others.

*Being Present is knowing the divine sacredness
and interconnection of all aspects of life:
minerals, plants, animals, human beings, solar
systems, galaxies, and multiverses.*

*Presence allows us to heal ourselves enough to
be happy by fulfilling our purpose in being here,
knowing that it is all right if everything
isn't healed.*

Presence teaches us to allow things that annoy us to pass through us rather than to resist them. Then the matter may no longer take our power away. Resistance results in unhappiness.

If we withdrew our Presence from Presence, we would not exist; nothing un-Present exists.

Our Presence knows we have the Present-power to transform and transcend any and all obstructions in our lives. When the student is ready, the teacher Presently appears.

By our Presence becoming aware of our emotions and thoughts, we can shift whatever we create in our lives.

The majority of humanity is never Present, and many of us vacillate between frequencies of Presence and non-Presence. Our destiny is to become Present, so let us begin by accepting where we are at Present.

Coming from a place of Presence, we can see another's physical, emotional, and mental bodies as a movie or play that we are not really in.

Being Present is me knowing I am good and worthy enough.

Our Presence wishes us to know that the unknown is the unknown; nothing is actually there other than our fear.

True Presence has no opposite.

❦

Presence allows us to know that our lives are simply about being Present.

Being conscious has no time; it lives in the Present and can produce great happiness.

Presence allows us to surrender to All There Is, and to be happy.

Nothing is more awe-inspiring than the inconceivable limitlessness of Presence.

Our Presence is our intention and commitment to be happy, which we may use to let go of all the old myths and behaviors surrounding ourselves that make us unhappy.

Our Presence allows us to accept and forgive all the ways that we have chosen to learn to love while coming here.

Through our freedom of choice and of will, we can choose Presence.

Our Presence knows that our truth lives within our knowing hearts and not within our believing heads.

❧

Our Presence knows that our feelings exist in every moment of the Present, but we are not them!

Presences allow us to use our energy for our highest good and to live our purpose.

Most relationships fail as a result of a lack of Presence.

All creation is the "being-ness" of Presence/ consciousness. This is what created everything, including you.

Our lack and limitation are learning tools to know Presence.

Presence is that part of us that ultimately stands alone as an individuated being, which values and loves who we are.

Let's stop trying to understand Presence and instead, just be it; Presence is not knowledge, it is ever-Present being.

Presence and creation are not separate. We are Present's present.

Presence allows us to know who we are beyond our physical bodies, minds, and emotions.

Can you see in each Present moment how you are using your talents and gifts, which are simply who you are and what you have to bring out into the world that makes you happy?

Presence is stillness, a portal, a vortex between you and creation.

Without Presence the mind often creates what it believes even if it is painful.

Our Presence is a key player in creating a new world that is Present and happy all the time.

*Our Presence is our gateway to happiness
through gratitude for what is.*

*Through being Present, we know that thinking
we are special, spiritual, or conscious can
create separation.*

Unhappiness often lives in the past and future; happiness's real chance to exist is at Present.

❦

Presence shows us that happiness is our true nature and state of being, not something that we need to achieve.

The future without Presence often creates unhappiness.

Only through being Present can you experience the divine and true beauty.

Being Present is knowing that whatever happens outside of you, you are love, and that is what matters. Your Presence is truth, and that is love of self and others.

❦

Being Present is knowing that you came here to be a light worker, whatever that means for you.

The more Presence we bring into our everyday life, the better we are able to handle things when they are not going so well. What is our Presence during normal and not so normal Present moments?

Beware of our physical, emotional, and mental selves; don't let them be all you are. You are Presently so much more!

Our Presence is the pathway to our divine soul plan, some are at the beginning, some in the middle, and some have arrived. We shall all get there Present by Present by Present.

To be Present is to not look for an outcome.

A moment without emotion or thought is one of being fully Present. Experiencing this is divine Presence: everything becomes still and the real we *appears.*

Our Presence facilitates us living our happy lives from our knowing hearts.

Our Presence supports our connecting with what is important to us, with our passion, with our purpose, and with that which affects us most.

Present Mantra: Wake up! Release our mental and emotional bodies. Be Present!

Being Present is clearing, cleansing, and releasing all that does not serve our highest good and impedes our happiness.

Our Presence knows that life was never about **me,** *but about* **we.**

Our Presence knows that the unknown is simply filled with possibilities and probabilities.

When the non-Present mental body reacts, be neutral, do nothing, and allow the Present just to be.

When some look out onto their pathway, they see nothing. Being Present, we know that nothing is truly there, except for our self being Present.

When our emotions or thoughts take over, we become unconscious, unaware, not Present, and often unhappy.

The mental body and the concept of time are eternally linked. Stop time, and you can quiet the mind trapped in the past and future. Your Presence knows there is only the Present.

Many of the things we think of as bias are often a refusal of the Present by focusing on what is not, rather than what is.

Within Presence, there is a deep-seated happiness that moves beyond anything good or bad.

Being Present is embodying all our Presence, the core aspect of ourselves.

There are neither shaming and blaming, nor judgment in Presence.

❧

Presence is life in a refined, re-defined frequency of self, transmitting into everything.

In every Present moment, check in with yourself, and ask: (1) Where am I? (2) What am I fully feeling? (3) What do I need? Stay focused with your inner-Presence, and allow the answers to come...

Being Present and happy is knowing your talents and gifts and bringing them out into the world...

The only thing essential in life's journey is the moment you are experiencing at Present; actually, that's all there ever is!

Being Present is escaping from our mental body, which creates resistance. Surrender through Presence is the end of the believing-mind being in control and the mind going back into service of the knowing-heart.

As old paradigms die, what remains is Presence to build the new paradigm upon.

Being Present is saying yes to what is, rather than to what is not.

Problems and solutions are actually aspects of the same thing that is Present.

Our Presence knows the attachments and addictions that no longer serve our highest good or are the best use of our energy; and it knows how to release them.

Our Presence knows that much of our unhappiness has been the result of our resistance to feeling our feelings and releasing them, considering that we are **not** *our feelings.*

The future is often a picture of the past. Becoming Present eliminates the past.

*Presence teaches us that happiness is not
dependent upon the outer world.*

❧

Presence knows that **Source** *is waiting for
humanity to awaken and to join in oneness.*

*Presence allows us to infuse our doing
with our being.*

*When we direct Presence outward, we are in
world creation; when we direct Presence inward,
we are creating "me."*

Presence knows what we love about our self and what we are ready to give to others.

Only presence can recognize Presence, and Presence is a process of inside out, not outside in.

The mental body's needs are ceaseless and cause fear and a constant desire that can never be satisfied. Only through moving into our Presence, can we quiet the mental body. Remember that your real higher-self does not live in your mental body; it lives in your Presence.

Our Presence mirrors our truth. If we wish to change the world outside us, we need to first change the world inside us.

Our true, eternal, unseen, and formless Presence is who we truly are; in Presence we already know this.

Presence reduces suffering (long term pain) and thus, resistance, which causes pain. We actually transcend suffering through Presence.

Our Presence allows us to ask, "What is going on out there? Why is this happening? How is this affecting me?"

Being Present means that we have entered the center of our hearts, a place where only Presence exists (not time).

Our soul plan is both the ancient, and the new, soul plan, which we choose to express through our Presence.

Our Presence is constantly asking, "Am I expressing who I am through my talents and gifts?"

There can be no enlightenment without Presence.

Presence is the individuated part of creation within us.

Being without Presence often feels like not being good or worthy enough.

Being Present allows the creation of a new world of equality, harmony, and balance.

Presence supports our decision to move from separation into oneness with life.

Presence is our soul plan embodied within us.

Our Presence is showing us that we are moving from cause and effect and karmic consequence to divine Presence.

A momentary sexual orgasm is the closest many people get to Presence. This is only a brief glimpse at Presence; our destiny is to be Present all the time.

Without Presence, things in our life can be considered negative, dramatic, and harmful which are really learning tools we create.

Presence teaches us that the real parts of us never die.

Many spiritual teachings have taught us that the Present is the true gift of life. Most of our negative notions need the past and future and cannot be maintained and sustained in the Present.

Being Present supports your purpose in being here and knowing why.

Presence knows that resistance and force are not strength. They are masks pretending to be strong.

Within Presence you can withdraw all the energy you need for life.

Give Presence to yourself, and know how it feels to be loved.

❧

We are living in a body; God lives in Presence, flowing through us all the time.

Presence knows that we are just one step away from something unbelievable through surrendering to what is.

Through Presence, the acceptance of pain prevents suffering. Presence does not transform the circumstance; it transforms you.

Being Present is your chance to use Presence-energy through your freedom of will to create the new, fully happy you.

❦

Presence is what makes us whole and complete, whether we are male or female, black or white, gay or straight, right or wrong, or weak or strong.

Presence enables our connection with oneness, with Source.

❦

Presence allows shame, blame, and judgment to cease and to be replaced by acceptance, compassion, and forgiveness.

Our Presence always supports who we truly are, free of the expectations of others.

Presence teaches us that when our addiction to the physical form is reduced, we become happier. People and things that we thought we needed to be happy come to us with grace and ease when we reduce expectation.

To become Present is our reason to be here.

*Through Presence our talents and gifts can
change the world.*

Being Present is discovering your purpose and knowing what resonates for you and what does not.

Presence knows we are indestructible, immortal beings of light that need no physical proof.

Our Presence is constantly showing us the path to be and to love ourselves.

∽

Presence is inclusive, not exclusive.

Through Presence we can accept what is and move from unhappiness to happiness

Our Presence is really who we are and the way to discovering why we are here.

Presence teaches us that there is neither negative nor positive; they are essences of the same thing.

Many people are not aware they have Presence. Some know they do. Which are you?

Presence is an in-depth way of listening by bypassing the mental and emotional bodies. Sense of Presence is all about reclaiming true Presence from our mental and emotional bodies.

Being Present is knowing the difference between expectations and accepting what is.

Being Present is knowing what responsibility and consequence mean: responsibility for self and for others.

Presence is not something outside you; it is inside you, waiting to go outside.

At Present, deceit and denial of deceit are common-place in our world and create much unhappiness. Presence knows that only through truth can we be happy.

Through Presence we know that all physical forms are impermanent; we see the relations between seen and unseen worlds.

Presence teaches us to build a parallel path, rather than to confront, resist, or fight.

Presence reveals there that is often a wounded little girl or boy leading our lives. Presence allows us to heal that child in order for us to become the happy adult in the Present.

Presence allows us to transform unconsciousness into consciousness.

Being Present will set us free right now.

Within Presence, the old paradigm of you and the world can become a new paradigm of being.

Presence eliminates the need for duality, separation, conflict, and war.

Only an un-Present person can be used and/or manipulated, and conversely, only an un-Present person will use or manipulate others.

Attempt to stay Present in all areas that your mental and emotional bodies wish to escape. By being Present, you are fully alive and not trying to escape life.

Being Present is knowing that all suffering is self-inflicted, for both ourselves and others.

Being Present is doing something that brings great happiness into your life.

Our Presence knows that we do not have to meet anyone else's expectations or prove anything outside of our Present self to be happy.

An emotion is a reaction to a thought from your mind. Emotions and thoughts create our life all the time. Presence frees us from both by allowing us to experience them and then to release them.

Being Present is fully being you without masks or ego-defenses, allowing you to be transparent and authentic.

Being Present allows a new you and a new soul family to be born, and for you both to connect with one another...

Our Presence wants to know where our truth comes from. Does it come from inside of us or from outside?

Being able to access our Presence on a Present-to-Present basis is the necessary new normal.

Resources

Phillip Elton Collins

The Angel News Network. www. theangelnewsnetwork.com

Coming Home to Lemuria: An Ascension Adventure Story. www.facebook.com/ComingHometoLemuria. (Order via: http://www.theangelnewsnetwork.com/ page22/ book-comingHome.html)

Sacred Poetry & Mystical Messages (www.facebook. com/SacredPoetryMysticalMessages. (Order via: http://www.theangelnewsnetwork.com/ book-sa-cred-poetry.html)

Manpower Godpower. (Order via: http://www.theangelnewsnetwork.com/ book- life-mastery.html)

Joel D. Anastasi

The Ascension Handbook. www.facebook. com/TheAscensionHandbookCreate-YourEcstaticUnionWithGod

(Order via: http://www.theangelnewsnetwork.
com/ascen- sion_handbook.html)

Life Mastery. https://www.facebook.com/
TheLifeMasteryProgram

The *Second Coming: Archangel Gabriel Proclaims a New
Age.* www.gabrielsecondcoming.com www.facebook.
com/GabrielTheSecondComing
(Order via: http://www.theangelnewsnetwork.com/
book- second-coming.html)

Jeff Fasano

www.journeyoftheawakenedheart.net www.facebook.
com/Journeyoftheawakenedheart
(Order via: http://www.theangelnewsnetwork.com/
page23/ book-journey.html)

www.ingramcontent.com/pod-product-compliance
Lightning Source LLC
Chambersburg PA
CBHW020845090426
42736CB00008B/246